Look, a Shark!

by Tessa Kenan

BUMBA BOOKS™

LERNER PUBLICATIONS ◆ MINNEAPOLIS

Note to Educators:

Throughout this book, you'll find critical thinking questions. These can be used to engage young readers in thinking critically about the topic and in using the text and photos to do so.

Lerner Publications Company
A division of Lerner Publishing Group, Inc.
241 First Avenue North
Minneapolis, MN 55401 USA

For reading levels and more information, look up this title at www.lernerbooks.com.

Library of Congress Cataloging-in-Publication Data

Names: Kenan, Tessa, author.
Title: Look, a shark! / by Tessa Kenan.
Description: Minneapolis : Lerner Publications, [2017] | Series: Bumba books—I see ocean animals | Audience: Age 4–8. | Audience: K to grade 3. | Includes bibliographical references and index.
Identifiers: LCCN 2015048776 (print) | LCCN 2016010653 (ebook) | ISBN 9781512414196 (lb : alk. paper) | ISBN 9781512415056 (pb : alk. paper) | ISBN 9781512415063 (eb pdf)
Subjects: LCSH: Sharks—Juvenile literature.
Classification: LCC QL638.9 .K45 2017 (print) | LCC QL638.9 (ebook) | DDC 597.3—dc23

LC record available at http://lccn.loc.gov/2015048776

Manufactured in the United States of America

1 – VP – 7/15/16

LERNER
SOURCE

Expand learning beyond the printed book. Download free, complementary educational resources for this book from our website, www.lernerresource.com.

Table of Contents

Sharks Swim

Sharks are fish.

They swim in oceans.

Sharks live all over the world.

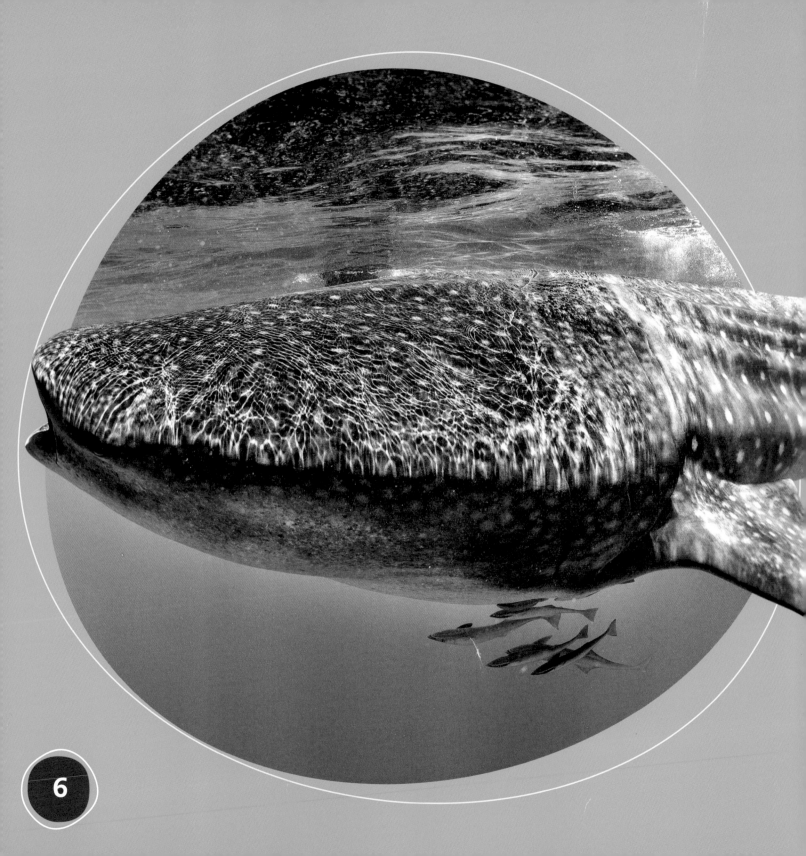

There are many kinds of sharks.

One is longer than a bus.

One is shorter than a ruler.

A shark has fins.

The back fin helps it swim.

The top fin helps it balance.

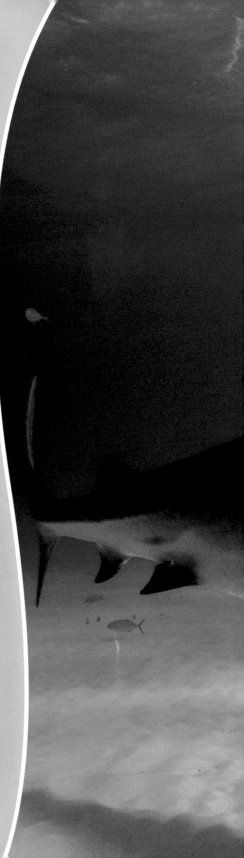

gills

Sharks have gills.

Gills help sharks breathe.

Sharks can smell in water too.

Smelling helps sharks find prey.

How could smelling help a shark find prey?

Sharks are darker on top.

This helps sharks hunt.

They blend in with the water below.

Animals near the surface cannot

see the sharks.

Shark bellies are a light color. The bellies blend in with the water above.

Why would a light belly be helpful for hunting?

Sharks have rows of teeth.

These teeth help sharks catch food.

Great white sharks can have 300 teeth!

How do you think sharp teeth help sharks hunt?

A whale shark eats with its

mouth open.

It catches small animals.

Baby sharks are

called pups.

Pups swim away from

their mother.

They take care

of themselves.

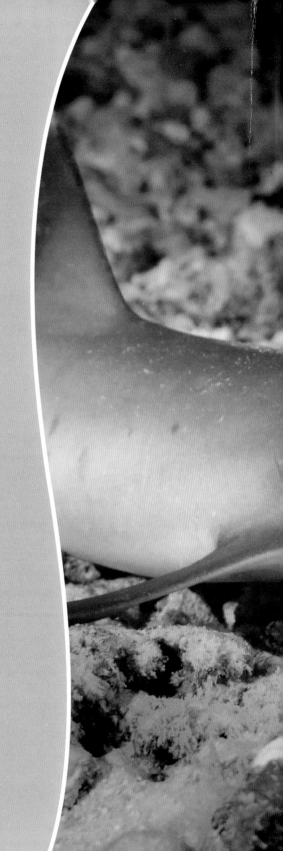

Parts of a Shark

eye

fins

snout

teeth

gills

22

Picture Glossary

gills

body parts that
help fish breathe

prey

animals that other animals
hunt and eat for food

pups

baby sharks

surface

the top layer
of water in an
ocean or lake

23

Index

Read More

Markovics, Joyce L. *Great White Shark.* New York: Bearport Publishing, 2016.

Meister, Cari. *Do You Really Want to Meet a Shark?* Mankato, MN: Amicus, 2016.

Nelson, Kristin L. *Let's Look at Sharks.* Minneapolis: Lerner Publications, 2011.

Photo Credits